D1737478

For my children. --- M.C.H.

Marshall likes to do many things.

He enjoys dancing.

running,

and reading,

The Origin of Grits

but most of all he likes to snack.

Marshall...

His mother would politely call out.

Nom, nom
nom, nom.

Marshall...

She called out again.

Mmmmm...

Tasty.

What are you doing?

Having a snack.

What are you snacking on?

Peas.

Ok.

Marshall...

Crunch, crunch
munchy, munch.

What are you doing?

Having a snack.

What are you snacking on?

A cucumber.

That's great!

Marshall...

Yum, yum
yummy, yum.

What are you doing?

Having a snack.

Marshall...

Chew, chew
chewy, chew.

Marshall

Yes ma'am?

What are you doing?

Having a snack.

What are you snacking on this time?

A chicken bone.

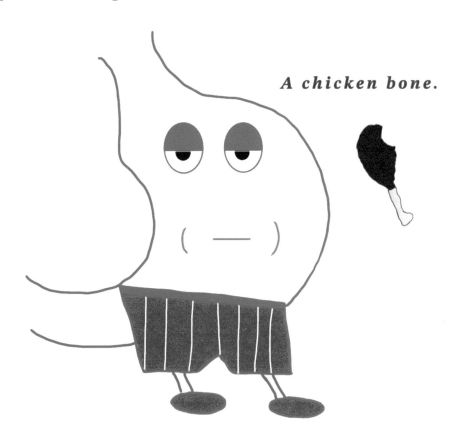

A chicken bone?!

Wait!

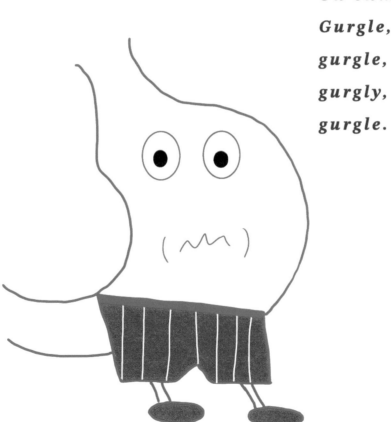

Uh oh...
Gurgle,
gurgle,
gurgly,
gurgle.

Bbbbuuuuu...

...*uuuuuRRRRRrrrRRR*...

...*uuuuurrrrrp.*

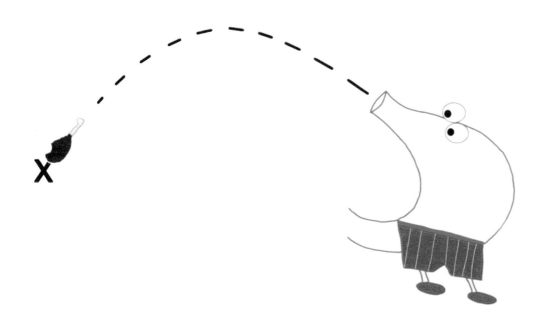

Excuse me.

Made in the USA
Columbia, SC
12 May 2024

35521297R00018